The Will According to Edwards and Girardeau

Doctrine of the Human Will

Martin Murphy

The Will According to Edwards and Girardeau

Copyright © 2020 by Martin Murphy

ISBN 9781733454032

To my wife, Mary
To the glory of God
In memory of
Dr. John Gerstner

Table of Contents

Introduction

This brief monograph on the human will examines the doctrinal conflicts of two great theologians on the doctrine of the will. Every decision you make whether conscious or unconscious comes from that aspect of the soul called the will. The will and the mind interface in the soul so as to constitute, with the emotions, the fullness of the human personality. The will has received so much discussion and debate over the past 2500 years that anything I say is not even a footnote. However, Jonathan Edwards and John Lafayette Girardeau devoted considerable energy on the doctrine of the human will.

This brief monograph may challenge some Christians, but it may motivate others to ponder the doctrine of the will. It may seem too academic for some laymen, but it will be worth the effort to muse and discover the doctrine of the will. However, every Christian should endeavor to investigate this important doctrine, because its centrality to Christian growth.

Jonathan Edwards gave as good of an explanation as any I've found or that I might conceive.

> The will (without any metaphysical refining) is plainly, that by which the mind chooses anything. The faculty of the will is that faculty or power of principle of mind by which it is capable of choosing: an act of the will is the same as an act of choosing or choice."

He goes on to say "A man never, in any instance, wills anything contrary to his desires, or desires anything contrary to his will. (*Freedom of the Will*, vol. 1, Yale edition, p. 137ff)

The nature of man after the fall is such that decisions or choices are either ungodly or godly choices. Christians have a renewed mind and a will that have the potential to make an ungodly choice or a godly choice. The Apostle Paul explains this unique doctrine. "And do not be conformed to this world, but be transformed by the renewing of your mind, that you may prove what is that good and acceptable and perfect will of God" (Romans 12:2). The will of the old nature is inclined to choose for self; self-gratification, self-fulfillment, self-esteem, self-worship, all of which are ungodly. The will of the new nature in Christ is inclined to choose for the love of God; it is a godly choice. The new man in Christ may make an ungodly choice, but he has the Holy Spirit, the Word of God, and the church to help him and show him the godly choice. Your choices come from your will; it will be worth the time and energy you spend learning more about the freedom or bondage of your will.

The Will According to Edwards and Girardeau

John Lafayette Girardeau was a church doctor, theologian, apologist, and minister of the gospel in the Southern Presbyterian Church. He lived and ministered prior to, during, and after the Civil War. Dr. Girardeau was Professor of Didactic and Polemic Theology at Columbia Theological Seminary from 1876 to 1895. As a church doctor, he was and still is recognized as a formidable contributor to the good health of the church. As a theologian, he left the church with a legacy in his theological writings. It is the purpose of this paper to interact with one of his least known theological writings, one that is primarily concerned with his metaphysical inquiry of the freedom of the will.

Dr. Girardeau wrote a series of articles which were later redacted by the author and published under the title, *The Will in it's Theological Relations*. This is a particularly unique treatise, because he takes issue with the work of Jonathan Edwards entitled *The Freedom of the Will*. Girardeau's work is unique, not just because he objects to Edward's view of the will, but that both men are Reformed, Calvinistic, and have the goal of crushing the Arminian argument in relation to the will. Theologically and apologetically both men are closer together than it might appear if their view of the will is the only consideration.

Girardeau seeks to vindicate Calvinism from a supposed dangerous philosophical school known as necessitarianism.

determinism is used as a synonym for necessitarianism. Although the critique of Edwards' understanding of the will, known as necessitarianism by Girardeau, is detailed, acute, presented with logical precision and lengthy, it appears that Girardeau has a deeper fear of the work of Edwards. This is detected when Girardeau states "the determining necessity of nature must be either a necessity of co-action (or force)"[1] and it is in the use of the word "force" that we find Girardeau's fundamental argument against necessity. The word "force" is the vulgar term for the more philosophical and theological word "fatalism." Girardeau pronounces his disdain against fatalism.

> [T]he Necessitarian doctrine of the necessary causality of the Supreme Being in all that he does, is at variance with the ordinary teachings of the Calvinistic theology; and fifthly, that the doctrine that all events, including the acts of the human will, come to pass by reason of a pre-determining and invincible necessity, is more fatalistic than that which has been held by some of the most distinguished Stoics themselves.[2]

---

[1]John L. Girardeau, *The Will in its Theological Relations* (New York: The Baker and Taylor Co., 1891) p. 302.

[2]Ibid., p. 318-319.

4

The necessitarian doctrine that Girardeau vehemently challenges does not at all belong to Edwards. It almost appears to be used pejoratively by Girardeau in his critique of *The Freedom of the Will* by Edwards. The school, which is commonly called necessitarianism, is the "theory that every event in the universe is determined by logical or causal necessity. . . .[and] as a theory of cosmic necessity, becomes in its special application to the human will, determinism."[3] Edwards explains that "a thing is. . .said to be necessary, when it must be, and cannot be otherwise."[4]

Fatalism is an entirely different and fatal concept. Some Calvinists have certainly been charged with fatalism, but they are false charges. "Fate is. . . a cosmic determinism that has no ultimate meaning or purpose"[5] and all Christians know very well that there is meaning and purpose in all that God ordains, wills, and executes in His wise providence. Fate destroys human freedom and God's providence.

---

[3]Dagobert D. Runes, ed., *Dictionary of Philosophy* (Totowa, New Jersey: Rowman And Allanheld, 1984), p. 223.

[4]Perry Miller, *The Works of Jonathan Edwards*, 9 vols. (New Haven: Yale University Press, 1957), vol. 1: The Freedom of the Will, p. 149.

[5]Walter A. Elwell, ed., *Evangelical Dictionary of Theology* (Grand Rapids: Baker Book House, 1984), p. 407.

Edwards expected sharp polemic disputes toward the "necessitarian" doctrine and its relation to the human will, but doubtful that he expected it from Calvinistic theologians such as Girardeau.

> Tis not unlikely, that some who value themselves on the supposed rational and generous principles of the modern fashionable divinity, will have their indignation and disdain raised at the sight of this discourse, and on perceiving what things are pretended to be proved in it. And if they think it worthy of being read,. . .may probably renew the usual exclamations, with additional vehemence and contempt, about the "fate" of the heathen, Hobbes' "necessity," and "making men mere machines"; accumulating the terrible epithets of "fatal,". . .and may be used to set forth things which have been said, in colors which shall be shocking to the imaginations. . .[6]

Henry Phillip Tappan wrote a review (very similar to Girardeau's review) entitled *A Review of Edwards's Inquiry into the Freedom of the Will*. This work was published in 1839 with these concluding words: "I finish my review of Edwards's system.. . .[W]hen we take a walk in the academian grove, I view him in a different character, and here his voice does not

---

[6] Jonathan Edwards, *Freedom of the Will*, p. 430.

6

sound to me so sweet as Plato's."[7] These men do not object to the love and passion with which Edwards defends the Christian religion, they are protesting against a philosophy that does not, to their mind, have a sound theological ground. Girardeau's argument against the "necessity" (or certainty) of the will as described by Edwards is not without a precise attempt to redefine the place of necessity in the whole argument. Girardeau quoted John Calvin to try to prove that Calvin's understanding of necessity was the same as his. Girardeau said that Calvin "opposes. . .a force acting against the will,"[8] but so does Jonathan Edwards. Calvin does make that statement, but it is unclear whether or not he intends it to mean prelapsarian or postlapsarian or man in his regenerate estate.

Calvin's references to God's eternal decrees, causality, and the will are so plentiful that his work would require a separate work of great depth. Calvin's references to God's eternal decrees, causality, and the will are so plentiful that his work would require a separate work of great depth. It is not the purpose here to grind out such complicated details, but only to

---

[7]Henry Phillip Tappan, *A Review of Edwards's Inquiry into the Freedom of the Will* (New York: John S. Taylor, 1839), p. 300.

[8]John L. Girardeau, *The Will in its Theological Relation*, p. 153.

7

establish Edwards' meaning of the word in its relationship to the Will. The words of Edwards are sufficient.

I use the word 'necessity' in the following discourse, when I endeavor to prove that necessity is not inconsistent with liberty. The subject and predicate of a proposition, which affirms existence of something, may have a full, fixed, and certain connection several ways.

(1) They may have a full and perfect connection in and of themselves; because it may imply a contradiction, or gross absurdity, to suppose them not connected. Thus many things are necessary in their own nature. So the eternal existence of being generally considered, is necessary in itself: because it would be in itself the greatest absurdity, to deny the existence of being in general, or to say there was absolute and universal nothing; and is as it were the sum of all contradictions; as might be shewn, if this were a proper place for it. So God's infinity, and other attributes are necessary. So it is necessary in its own nature, that two and two should be four; and it is necessary, that all right lines drawn from the center of a circle to the circumference should be equal. It is necessary, fit and suitable, that men should do to others, as they would that they should do to them. So innumerable metaphysical and mathematical truths are necessary in themselves.

(2) The connection of the subject and predicate of a proposition, which affirms the existence of something, may be fixed and made certain, because the existence of that thing is already come to pass; and either now is, or has been; and so has as it were made sure of existence. And there, the proposition, which affirms present and past existence of it, may by this means be made certain, and necessarily and unalterably true; the past event has fixed and decided the matter, as to its existence; and has made it impossible but that existence should be truly predicated of it. Thus the existence of whatever is already come to pass, is now become necessary; (my emphasis) 'tis impossible it should be otherwise than true, that such a thing has been.

(3) The subject and predicate of a proposition which affirms something to be, may have a real and certain connection consequentially; and so the existence of the thing may be consequentially necessary;. . .Things which are perfectly connected with other things that are necessary, are necessary themselves, by a necessity of consequence.[9]

---

[9] Jonathan Edwards, *Freedom of the Will*, p. 152-153.

Girardeau is distraught by the Edwardsian concept of necessity in its relation to the will of Adam in his sinless estate. Girardeau explains his complaint:

> [A] power of contrary choice, which the Determinist utterly denies, and which, in relation to the contrasts of sin and holiness, is precisely that freedom of the will (*liberum arbitrium*) which was lost by the Fall, and the loss of which has reduced man to the moral necessity of choosing only one alternative – the fatal one of sin. So far from having been a rigorous a Determinist as Jonathan Edwards, in regard to man in innocence, Calvin taught that in that estate he possessed a freedom of the will other than that of spontaneity, and inconsistent with necessity; that is the liberty of contrary choice, which the Determinist wholly denies.[10]

The argument between these two great divines will not end until a proper distinction can be made between the use of the word necessity and its relationship to the will of man, both in his sinless estate, unregenerate estate, and his regenerate

---

[10]John L. Girardeau, *The Will in its Theological Relation*, p. 157 - 158.

10

estate. Dr. John Gerstner, noted scholar and recognized authority on the works of Jonathan Edwards explains:

> A necessary act of the will is popularly supposed to be its acting in spite of its own inclination to the contrary. This is not the case, according to Edwards. A thing or an act can be necessary with no presumed opposition. For example, the very eternal existence of God is necessary.[11]

Edwards clearly described what his intended double meaning of the word "necessity" (moral and natural) was in The Freedom of the Will. Where Edwards gave eight pages to explain in great detail the meaning of the word necessity, Girardeau gave less than one half a page. Girardeau's argumentation would have been much more effective if he had devoted more effort toward the definition of the key words used in his argument, especially the use of the words necessity and liberty.

Girardeau assumes that the "liberty of contrary choice" is exclusive of a necessary act. Why was Girardeau so preoccupied with the necessitarian school? The answer is

---

[11]John H. Gerstner, *The Rational Biblical Theology of Jonathan Edwards*, vol. 2 (Berea Publications: Powhatan, Virginia and Ligonier Ministries: Orlando, Fla. 1992), p. 177.

found in his own question. "Did God decree so to order and dispose Adam's case as to render his sin necessary, without himself proximately producing it?"[12] It is an age old question. If God decrees everything, does His decree include sin? How did sin enter the human race? There is not an easy answer to this profound question. Edwards and Girardeau would both deny that God is the doer of sin, but Girardeau argues that Edwards' system has a hole in it and that his system tends to make God the cause of sin. Edwards on the other hand would say that God decreed sin, but He does not do sin. The Westminster divines did not waste much print upon the matter. Their brief, but compelling answer was that "God was pleased, according to his wise and holy counsel, to permit, having purposed to order it to his own glory."[13] The mystery questions "why" and "how" are left to God's own glory. The predestinating power of God does not calm the inquiring philosophical and theological mind of Edwards or Girardeau. In fact that only begins the debate. The hypothetical charge by Girardeau against the allegedly deterministic Edwards is primarily rooted in Girardeau's understanding or lack of it or

---

[12]John L. Girardeau, *The Will in its Theological Relation*, p. 64.

[13]*Westminster Confession of Faith* (Glasgow: Free Presbyterian Publications, 1985). p. 38.

his disagreement with the law of causality. He charges the necessitarians with inconsistency within their own system. He uses the *ad hominem* argument thus:

> All creaturely causes derive, as second causes, their necessity from the necessary causality of the First Cause. If not, how are necessary second causes, as effects, to be accounted for? They surely cannot be consistently assigned an absolute beginning. They must be referred to God as the first, the original and determining First Cause. If so, the necessary causality of God operated, though the agency of man as a necessary cause, to the production of the first sin. It does not relieve the difficulty to say that man was the proximate cause, if God, through the remote, was the real cause.. . .The series of necessary second causes is a series of effects, and the first of the series is immediately connected with the efficiency of God as the First Cause.[14]

If Girardeau has correctly stated the argument, then a contradiction results. In fact Girardeau says the choice is either to go "with the doctrine of the Church, or with the

---

[14]John L. Girardeau, *The Will in its Theological Relation*, p. 294 - 295.

necessitarian philosophy?"[15] Girardeau implies that necessitarian philosophy and the doctrine of the church are contradictory. There is no reason not to believe that if the two appear contradictory, they could not be really reconciled. The possibility exists that the two may not be contradictory. Edwards is very careful to define the meaning of the word "cause" in this argument.

> Therefore I sometimes use the word "cause," in this inquiry, to signify any antecedent, either natural or moral, positive or negative, on which an event, either a thing, or the manner and circumstance of a thing, so depends, that it is the ground and reason, either in whole, or in part, why it is, rather than not; or why it is as it is, rather than otherwise; or, in other words, any antecedent with which a consequent event is so connected, that it truly belongs to the reason why the proposition which affirms that event, is true; whether it has any positive influence or not. . .Having thus explained what I mean by cause, I assert, that nothing ever comes to pass without a cause. What is self-existent must be from eternity, and must be unchangeable. . .That whatsoever begins to be, which before was not, must have a cause why it then begins

---

[15]Ibid., p. 295.

to exist, seems to be the first dictate of the common and natural sense which God hath implanted in the minds of all mankind, and the main foundation of all reasonings about the existence of things, past, present, or to come.[16]

Girardeau's contradiction disappears if Edwards has correctly defined the law of causality and correctly applied the law to the will. It must be remembered that the heart of the argument that brings causality to the front lines is to explain how God can decree sin and sin can come into existence through Adam without God being the cause of sin. Girardeau charges Edward's view of causality with making God not only the author of sin, but also the doer of sin. Edwards does teach that God ordains sin and in a sense if God ordains it he causes it. Edwards explains:

Tis true, as was observed before, there is no effect without some cause, occasion, ground or reason of that effect, and some cause answerable to the effect. But certainly it will not follow. . .that a transient effect

---

[16]Jonathan Edwards, *Freedom of the Will*, p. 180-181.

requires a permanent cause, or a fixed influence and propensity. [O]ne act don't prove a fixed inclination. [17]

Edwards may have stumbled here because the origin of Adam's inclination to sin is not answered in Scripture or in philosophy. Edwards argues that the inclination to sin existed in Adam's will, but it does not have to be proved that the inclination was a "fixed" or a "permanent" inclination. Girardeau appeals to the Westminster divines to confirm his hypothesis. The *Westminster Confession of Faith* posits:

> God from all eternity did, by the most wise and holy counsel of his own will, freely, and unchangeably ordain whatsoever comes to pass: yet so, as thereby neither is God the author of sin, nor is violence offered to the will of the creatures, nor is the liberty of contingency of second causes taken away, but rather established. [18]

Girardeau believed that necessary and contingent causes are, to their nature, expressly distinguished from each other.

---

[17]Perry Miller, *The Works of Jonathan Edwards*, 9 vols. (New Haven: Yale University Press, 1957), vol. 3: Original Sin, p. 191.

[18]*Westminster Confession of Faith*, p. 28.

He is correct, but the confession does not define the specific contingences in relationship to the creatures. If God decrees all things and Girardeau would certainly agree to that, then was it possible for Him to decree for Adam to sin and not sin at the same time? Absolutely not. Was God's decree contingent upon Adam's volition? Absolutely not. Gerstner explains contingency as Edwards used it:

> Contingency, for Edwards, was one of Arminianism's major errors. Strictly speaking, the term means that events touch on each other or are inter-connected one leading to the next, which causally follows. But under the very term "contingency" that concept was denied by the Arminians. For them, volitional events were independent of each other, such events being resolved by the will free ('free will') without any anterior cause. This Edwards supposed with all the force of his *Freedom of the Will* under the heading of contingency meaning Arminian contingency, which was really a denial of the meaning of contingency. Effects, according to Edwards, follow antecedent causes and do not arise by spontaneous generation.[19]

---

[19]John H. Gerstner, *The Rational Biblical Theology of Jonathan Edwards*, p. 156.

The existence and operation of contingent causes are ordained and established by God, but it is the "second causes" that appear to be a spontaneous act of the creature. *The Westminster Confession* further clarifies the use of second causes.

> Although, in relation to the foreknowledge and decree of God, the first cause, all things come to pass immutably and infallibly; yet, by the same providence, he ordereth them to fall out according to the nature of second causes, either necessarily, freely, or contingently.[20]

A. A. Hodge agrees with Edwards against Girardeau that "God's decree includes and determines the means and conditions upon which events depend, as well as the events themselves."[21] The only contingencies in the mind of God are those contingencies that He ordained. Hodge goes on to say that God "controls his creatures and their actions, and effects his purposes through them. . .perfectly consistent with the nature of the creature and of his action."[22]

---

[20]*Westminster Confession of Faith*, p. 34.

[21]A. A. Hodge, *The Confession of Faith*. (Carlisle, Penn.: Banner of Truth Trust, 1958), p. 67.

[22]Ibid., p. 95.

Girardeau does not deny the law of causality in his argument against Edwards. Girardeau said:

the difference came in the nature of second causes: We affirming that some are necessary and others are contingent, and the reviewer obliterating this distinction and maintaining that all second causes, as media through which the divine efficiency exerts itself, are characterized by necessity.[23]

The resolution to this controversy will end when a theologian can truthfully, logically, theologically, philosophically, and necessarily answer the question: "Is the will necessarily determined, or not?"[24]

Adam's will was necessarily determined to sin, because God permitted the sin that Adam necessarily determined. Girardeau does not like that kind of language and tries to overstate the "distinction between efficacious and permissive

---

[23]John L. Girardeau, *The Will in its Theological Relation*, p. 182.

[24]Henry Phillip Tappan, *A Review of Edwards's Inquiry into the Freedom of the Will*, p. 196.

19

decrees."[25] There is a distinction between these two concepts, but there is a sense (no contradiction) in which they are similar. John Calvin offers this explanation:

> [T]he Psalmist sings, "The Lord hath done in heaven whatsoever pleased Him." This, however, is not true, if He willed some things and did them not. Nothing, therefore, is done but that which the Omnipotent willed to be done, either by permitting it to be done or by doing it Himself nor is a doubt to be entertained that God does righteously in permitting all those things to be done which are done evilly. For He permits not this, but by righteous judgment. Although, therefore, those things, which are evil, in so far as they are evil, are not good, yet it is good that there should not only be good things, but evil also. . . .Unless we fully believe this the very beginning of our faith is periled, by which we profess to believe in God ALMIGHTY!"[26]

---

[25] John L. Girardeau, *The Will in its Theological Relation*, p. 185.

[26] John Calvin, *Calvin's Calvinism: Treatises on the Eternal Predestination of God and the Secret Providence of God*, trans. Henry Cole (Grand Rapids: Reformed Free Publishing Association) p. 43.

Girardeau maintains that "God neither decreed efficiently to produce the sin of Adam, nor efficaciously to procure its commission, nor to render it unavoidable by a consecrated necessity of nature; but that he decreed to permit it."[27] It does not matter that God's decrees are efficacious or permissive, their causal agency must be substantiated. God's permissive decree as a first cause is perfectly agreeable with God's permissive decree as a second cause. A permissive decree does not imply that God's will was conditioned by a contingency. Calvin's affirmation is accompanied by other great theologians of the seventeenth century Reformation.

> The decree is ascribed to God not inasmuch as it is the effect of previous deliberation and consultation with reasoning passing from one thing to another (of which he has no need to whose eyes all things are naked and most open, Heb. 4:13), but by reason of the certain determination concerning the futurition of things (according to which the Psalmist sings, "The Lord hath done in heaven whatsoever pleased Him." This, however, is not true, if He willed some things and did them not. Nothing, therefore, is done but that which the Omnipotent willed to be done, either by permitting

---

[27]John L. Girardeau, *The Will in its Theological Relation*, p. 183.

it to be done or by doing it Himself. Nor is a doubt to be entertained that God does righteously in permitting all those things to be done which are done evilly. For He does nothing rashly, but designedly, i.e. knowingly and willingly).[28]

Girardeau looks for a way to escape the inevitable charge that God's decrees are designed, known, and willed by seeking safe ground on God's permissive decrees. His escape is to say that "the permitted events themselves, so far as the intrinsic causal agency of the creature is concerned, may be contingent, that is, so far as that intrinsic agency is concerned, not necessary and unavoidable."[29] The intrinsic nature of man is inseparably related to the moral agency of man, so how could it have been any different in Adam? If we try to escape his charge, we fall right in the lap of the Arminian. It sounds as if Girardeau says that permissively decreed events may be

---

[28]Francis Turretin, *Institutes of Elenctic Theology*, 3 vols. trans. George Musgrave Giger. ed. James T. Dennison, Jr. (Phillipsburg: Presbyterian and Reformed Publishing, 1992), p. 311.

[29]John L. Girardeau, *The Will in its Theological Relation*, p. 298.

avoided. At this point Girardeau's Calvinism has been distorted because the Arminian doctrine is driven by volitions coming from uncaused events or effects. When pressed further with the question of necessity Girardeau responds:

> There is no other way, to our mind, in which the paradox can be explained, that, although God only permitted the sin of the first man and of the angels, as sin, he at the same times made its commission necessary and unavoidable. He did not necessitate it, in itself considered, but simply as an accident of a necessary act of event.[30]

Girardeau's inquiry has driven him to a point of confusion. An event, (Adams first sin) cannot be "not necessary and unavoidable" and a "necessary act" at the same time in the same relationship. This is not sensible to the mind, either from Scripture or reason. From this one point alone, it may be evident that Girardeau was not consistently keeping on track with his argument against Edwards. It is to be noted that Girardeau's essays appeared over a period of several years. It is plausible to think that Girardeau was laboring without the benefit of continuity and consistency.

---

[30] Ibid., p. 240.

The argument for the first sin being "the liberty of contrary choice" rather than an efficacious decree of God is liberally contended by Girardeau against the supralapsarians. He correctly argues that supralapsarianism teaches that God decreed to permit the first sin and because he decreed it He necessitated its commission. This argument is an extension of his polemic against necessitarianism and vigorously argues that Edwards is a necessitarian. The way Girardeau chronologically and logically presents his case, it would be safe to assume that Girardeau implies that Edwards is supralapsarian. It is simply not true, because Edwards was not a supralapsarian. Dr. John Gerstner has identified Edwards as an infralapsarian and gives a lengthy quote taken from *Remarks on Important Theological Controversies.*

> Hence God's decree of the eternal damnation of the reprobate is not be conceived of as prior to the fall, yea, and to the very being of the persons, as the decree of the eternal glory of the elect is. For God's glorifying his love, and communicating his goodness, stands in the place of a mere or ultimate end, and therefore is prior in the mind of the eternal Disposer of the very being of the subject, and to everything but mere possibility. . . . .Indeed the glorifying of God's mercy, as it presupposes the subject to be miserable, and the glorifying his grace, as it presupposes the subject to be sinful, unworthy, and ill deserving, are not to be conceived of as ultimate ends, but only as certain ways

and means for the glorifying the exceeding abundance and overflowing fullness of God's goodness and love; therefore these decrees are not to be considered as prior to the decree of the being and permission of the fall of the subject.[31]

The evidence compellingly favors Edwards the infralapsarian. Even so, Edwards insists that God's permissive decree necessarily required it commission.

Divine knowledge weighed heavily upon Girardeau's mind as he struggled to understand the will of Adam before the fall. Of particular importance was his understanding of God's foreknowledge in relation to the first sin of Adam. Girardeau argued that "whether God causally determined the certainty of the predicted events, the argument from prophecy is not logically concerned."[32] He constructs the view that Adam's first sin was not the object of prophecy. It is difficult to follow Girardeau's reasoning at this point, because biblical prophecy is not the issue at this point, except to establish that God's

---

[31]John H. Gerstner, *The Rational Biblical Theology of Jonathan Edwards*, p. 154.

[32] John L. Girardeau, *The Will in its Theological Relation*, p. 269.

prophecy is based on His foreknowledge. Girardeau tries to make a case that prophecy is analogous to the foreknowledge of God in relation to Adam's first sin. Edwards did draw an analogy between prophecy and foreknowledge as a biblical and theological foundation. Girardeau uses fallacious argumentation against Edwards:

> All the predicted sinful acts of sinful men were made certain by God; the first sin of Adam was the unpredicted sinful act of an innocent man; therefore the first sin of Adam was made certain by God: this precise statement of the argument is sufficient to evince its invalidity. There is no recorded prophecy of Adam's first sin, and therefore his free act in sinning is exempted from the scope of this argument from prophecy. We do not mean to imply that God could not have predicted Adam's first sin. But he did not.[33]

His fatal mistake is in the premise "the first sin of Adam was unpredicted." As a matter of biblical revelation Girardeau is correct, but it is established that God predicts many things that are not recorded in Scripture. God's foretelling is based on his foreordination on which his foreknowledge depends. The reason God knows in advance is because God plans in

---

[33]John L. Girardeau, *The Will in its Theological Relation*, p. 270.

advance. Girardeau offers insufficient theological and logical reasons for his argument that God knew that Adam must sin.

> To say that God certainly foreknew that Adam would sin, is one thing; it is quite another thing to say that God certainly foreknew the he must sin, inconsequence of the operation of necessary causes.[34]

The implication Girardeau makes in this one statement contradicts the aseity of God. The nature and character of God's eternal Being is such that He must have known that Adam would and therefore must sin, just as He must know by necessity the exact location of all sub-atomic particles at every point of time. The uncertainty that Girardeau propounds is out of keeping with the orthodox doctrine of the foreknowledge of God.

The importance of foreknowledge in relation to the will is given no small amount of attention by Girardeau. His declaration is summarized in this one statement. "His [God's] eternity is one undivided whole - he eternally is, and he eternally knows."[35] Girardeau would have favored his argument if he left it there. The relationship between the will and the mind is most important to Girardeau's argument.

---

[34]Ibid., p. 315-316.
[35]Ibid., p. 366

Will is our capacity to make choices, commitments, and decisions. Philosophers have often debated whether the intellect or the will is "primary." Do we make choices based on our knowledge, or does our knowledge arise from a choice to believe?[36]

John Frame has asked the question that Girardeau should have asked. What did Edwards have to say in this regard?

I speak not now of the certainty of knowledge, but the certainty that is in things themselves, which is the foundation of the certainty of the knowledge of them; or that wherein lies the ground of the infallibility of the proposition which affirms them."[37]

Edwards returns to the eternal decrees of God as the foundation for the will to act and the mind to correspondingly participate in the action. The epistemology of Girardeau needs fine tuning before his arguments will stand.

---

[36]John M. Frame, *The Doctrine of the Knowledge of God* (Phillipsburg: Presbyterian and Reformed Publishing Co., 1987), p. 343.

[37]Jonathan Edwards, *Freedom of the Will*, p. 153.

Dr. Girardeau labored to defend Calvinism against Arminianism. Edwards no less did the same. Both men are scholars and should be read by critical minds. It is easy to be a spectator in a game, but may be very difficult to play in a game. To read the work of Girardeau and Edwards on the will is not difficult, but the real task is to read them in light of the history and development of their critiques. These men were in the difficult arena where few men tread. Their minds were captivated by what appears to be the Achilles heel of Christianity that is God's sovereignty and the problem of evil. The doctrine of theodicy is not the most popular subject. Investigating the fall of Adam becomes increasingly difficult as the inquiry continues. Edwards uses the propositions of necessity and causality while Girardeau uses the proposition of the power of contrary choice. Who is correct? How did righteous Adam introduce sin into the human race without having a prior inclination to sin? These complicated questions are neatly tucked under the cover for the present. The mystery of God's inscrutable will in this matter is yet to appear to his chosen race. Dr. Girardeau and President Edwards and all other Christians agree with Dr. Girardeau's closing comment to Adam's race.

A conflict ensues, the result of which will be that his [the elect's] renewed will, being rendered immutable in consequence of Christ's fulfillment of the covenant as his Federal Representative, and of the determining grace of the Holy Spirit, will ultimately triumph, his sinful [nature] will be ultimately destroyed, and his whole perfected and glorified personality shall, in heaven, be indefectibly consecrated to the service and enjoyment of God.[38]

---

[38]John L. Girardeau, *The Will in its Theological Relation*, p. 485.

About the Author

Martin Murphy has a B.A. in Bible from Columbia International University and Master of Divinity from Reformed Theological Seminary. Martin spent nearly thirty years in the class room, the pulpit, the lectern, the study, and the library. He now devotes most of his time consolidating academic and practical gains by writing Christian books. He is the author of 18 Christian books on topics such as apologetics, theology, and biblical exposition. He and his wife Mary live in Dothan, Alabama.

More Books by Martin Murphy

The Church: First Thirty Years, 344 pages, ISBN 9780985618179, $15.95. This book is an exposition of the Book of Acts. It will help Christians understand the purpose, mission, and ministry of the church.

The Dominant Culture: Living in the Promised Land, 172 pages, ISBN 970991481118, $11.95. This book examines the culture of Israel during the period of the Judges. It explains how worldviews influence the church and it reveals biblical principles to help Christians learn how to live in the culture.

My Christian Apology, 98 pages, ISBN 9780984570874, $7.95. This book investigates the doctrine of Christian apologetics. It explains rational Christian apologetics.

The Essence of Christian Doctrine, 200 pages, ISBN 9780984570812, $12.95. This book was written so that pastors and layman would have a quick reference to major biblical doctrines. Dr. Steve Brown says it was written, "with clarity and power about the verities of the Christian faith and in a way that makes a difference in how we live."

Hosea Commentary: Return to the Lord, 130 pages, ISBN 9780984570805, $8.95. This book is an exposition Hosea. The prophet speaks a message of repentance and hope. Hosea's prophetic message to Old Testament and New Testament congregation is "you have broken God's covenant; return to the Lord. Dr. Richard Pratt said "We need more correct and practical instruction in the prophetic books, and you have given us just that."

Theological Terms in Layman Language, 130 pages, ISBN 9780985618155, $8.95. This book is written so that simple words like faith or not so simple words like aseity are explained in plain language. Theological Terms in Layman Language is easy to read and designed for people who want a brief definition for theological terms. The terms are in layman friendly language.

Brief Study of the Ten Commandments, 164 pages, 9780991481163, $10.95. This book will help Christians discover or re-discover the meaning of the Ten Commandments.

The Present Truth, 164 pages, ISBN 9780983244172, $8.95. Each chapter examines a topic relative to the Christian life. Topics such as church, sin, anger, marriage, education and more.

Doctrine of Sound Words: Summary of Christian Theology, 424 pages, ISBN 9780991481125, $16.95. This explains the doctrine of Christianity in a systematic format for the layperson. It covers a wide range of theological topics such as, the triune God, creation, providence, sin, justification, repentance, Christian liberty, free will, marriage and divorce, Christian fellowship, et al). There are thirty three topics beginning with "Holy Scriptures" and ending with "The Last Judgment." It is a systematic theology for laymen based on the full counsel of God.

The god of the Church Growth Movement, 95 pages ISBN 9780986405587, $6.95. This work includes a brief explanation of modernity and its effect on church growth. It is a critical analysis of the church growth movement found in every branch of the Protestant church.

Friendship: The Joy of Relationships, 46 pages, ISBN 9780986405518, $6.49. This condensed book was written so the reader will be able to grasp the principles without having to go back and re-read it to digest the content. Friendship is a popular concept. Having a large number of friends was popularized by the social media such as Twitter and Facebook. Friendship involves a relationship of distinction. It is a relationship that respects the dignity of another person. The Bible teaches a different version of what it means to be a friend than the popular culture teaches.

Ultimate Authority for the Soul, 151 pages, ISBN 9780986405501, $9.99. This book examines that question and concludes that every rational being has some recognition of God as the ultimate authority. Although God is the ultimate authority, He confers His authority by means of the Word of God. The author examines Psalm 119 to build a defense for the ultimate authority for the soul.

Constitutional Authority in a Postmodern Culture, ISBN 9780985618124, 56 pages, $5.95. This book shows the validity of constitutional authority and the invasion of postmodern theories in western culture. Postmodern theory has assaulted the western culture on the battleground of absolute truth and reality. Postmodern theory places human experience over abstract objective principles. Christians have a constitution known as the Bible so they will know the truth of reality. The last chapter is devoted to cultural reformation.

Learn to Pray: Biblical Doctrine of Prayer, ISBN 9780986405563, 107 pages, $7.95. This book examines the Lord's model prayer so Christians may learn to pray according to the Lord's instruction. It also reviews some of the prayers of the apostle Paul to discover his doctrine of prayer. Pastor James Perry wrote the Foreword with insight and experience. "I am impressed with this book on the subject of Learn to Pray. It is stated briefly and succinctly following the model and example of the Lord's Prayer. There is considerable practical instruction on the meaning and implication about purposeful and biblical prayer and it will serve as a useful primer for all who apply the prayer principles. The reader will doubtlessly return to the instruction frequently for the practical help it offers."

God's Grace For the Church: Exposition of Ephesians, ISBN 9781732437906, 150 pages, $8.95. This exposition of Paul's letter to the church at Ephesus is readable, reasonable, and relevant. It brings the grace of God to the forefront of the Christian experience. The author simply lays out the plain teaching of Scripture. Martin does not avoid theological topics that are obviously in the text of Scripture, but he does not engage in contentious arguments. It is written for Christians who want to understand and experience the manifestation of God's grace. Pastor Clark Cornelius describes the book from a pastor's perspective. "With the storytelling of a historian, the compassion of a pastor, and the skill to make theology apply to daily living, Martin Murphy's Exposition of Ephesians guides the reader through a treasure house enumerating God's grace. It illuminates God's spiritual riches to a modern Church, which has forgotten Christ's wall-destroying work of unity. Murphy's work sounds the call for the modern Christian to embrace his pre-destiny, suit up for service, and enjoy God's gifts of grace and peace."